Camino Inglés: Ferrol to Santiago on Spain's English Way
Matthew Harms, Anna Dintaman, David Landis
Second edition, 2023

Copyright ©2018-2023 Village to Village Press, LLC
Village to Village® is a registered trademark of Village to Village Press, LLC.

Village to Village Press, LLC, Harrisonburg, VA, USA
www.villagetovillagepress.com

Photographs/Diagrams
All photographs and diagrams © Village to Village Press, LLC

Cover Photographs by Matthew Harms and David Landis
Front: Dirt path outside Fene
Back (left to right): The "Bosque Encantado," Santiago Cathedral, Boats on the Eume Rive
Inside title page: Iglesia de Santiago de Sigrás

ISBN: 978-1-947474-21-5
Library of Congress Control Number: 2018909338

Text, photographs, images and diagrams © Village to Village Press, LLC, 2018-2023
Map data based on openstreetmap.org, © OpenStreetMap contributors
Cover and book design by David Landis

Disclaimer: *Every reasonable effort has been made to ensure that the information contained in this book is accurate. However, no guarantee is made regarding its accuracy or completeness. Reader assumes responsibility and liability for all actions in relation to using the provided information, including if actions result in injury, death, loss or damage of personal property or other complications.*

Note about town names: We generally use the Spanish name for cities and towns, though most also have a name or spelling in the local language. We occasionally use the local language name when it is the most prominent.

This **map guidebook** is designed to be lightweight and minimalist. It provides detailed stage and city maps, lodging, services, and basic preparation, background information, and tips ☀. This book does not include comprehensive route descriptions, extensive historical background information, nor all hotel listings.

Visit **caminoguidebook.com** for more information. ⬈

Contents

The Camino Inglés

The Camino Inglés is a pilgrimage route in northwestern Spain beginning from Ferrol or A Coruña and culminating at the cathedral in Santiago de Compostela, where St. James is believed to be buried. Many think of the "Camino" as the Francés route, traversing from St-Jean-Pied-de-Port to Santiago. In reality, there are many Caminos, echoing the ancient roads that pilgrims trod from all over Europe to Santiago. The Camino Inglés was traditionally the route taken by pilgrims from Northern Europe, Britain, and Ireland—hence the name "English Way." These pilgrims first sailed to seaports in northwest Spain before continuing by foot to Santiago. While A Coruña was a popular starting point, most pilgrims today start from Ferrol since A Coruña is less than 100km from Santiago so does not earn the walker a Compostela. Only 115km from Ferrol (or 73km from A Coruña), the Camino Inglés is the shortest of the modern Camino routes—a nice option for those short on time or intimidated by the physical demands of longer Camino journeys. Some towns and stages have inadequate albergue beds to match demand in the higher seasons, but hotels and guesthouses have stepped in to offer pilgrim rates. Because the Inglés has fewer pilgrims, the route also has had fewer improvements and utilizes paved surfaces more than the Francés (around 69% of the route from Ferrol). The upside of fewer walkers means more solitude and less overcrowding.

Saint James

In the New Testament, St. James is referred to as a disciple of Jesus who left his trade as a fisherman to follow Jesus. The Bible tells us little about him, save that he requested to be seated at the right hand of Jesus in heaven and was present at many events such as the Transfiguration and the Garden of Gethsemane. The last biblical mention of James is of his martyrdom in 44CE. St. James became known as the patron saint of Spain not from biblical account, but from tradition, oral history, legend and myth. The story goes that James preached in Iberia with little success. Mary appeared to James with the pillar to which Jesus was tied to be whipped and instructed him to build a church in Zaragoza. Shortly after his encounter with Mary, James returned to Jerusalem and was martyred, and his body was transported to Spain on a stone ship. The ship landed at Iria Flavia (Padrón), and James' disciples met the ship there to his body to be buried on a nearby hill. The body was forgotten until 813CE when a Christian hermit saw a light that led him to the grave. The bishop authenticated these relics, and King Alfonso II built a chapel to the saint. The event that catapulted this modest shrine to a major pilgrimage site was the mythical Battle of Clavijo in 852, when St. James was said to have appeared to assist the Christian army against Muslim invaders. This image of St. James was a convenient motif to draw Christian support to the frontier of Christian-Muslim battle and to bolster interest and financial investment in maintaining Christian domination of Iberia. The current cathedral was completed in the 1120s.

Camino Inglés
The English Way

Golfo Ártabro

Ferrol •

1

2 • Neda

Pontedeume • 3

1A • A Coruña

Betanzos • 4

Sergude • 2A

Hospital
de Bruma • 5

6

Sigüero •

• Santiago de
Compostela

The Camino Experience

The Camino de Santiago is a network of historical pilgrimage routes throughout Europe that lead to Santiago de Compostela in Spain, the traditional burial place of Saint James. Rather than a remote wilderness trek, the Camino weaves through villages, towns and even large cities. Walkers need not carry a heavy pack since frequent hostels and restaurants mean you can forego a tent, sleeping bag, and food resupply. The more popular Camino routes are well-trodden enough that you can be practically guaranteed walking companions in any season other than winter.

Many undertake the Appalachian, Pacific Crest Trail, or similar for wilderness and solitude, neither of which are primary experiences on the Camino, which offers camaraderie, encounters with culture and history, and, for many, a spiritual experience. Since the Camino routes were used for religious pilgrimage, any walker is generally considered a pilgrim, even if walking more for sport than spirituality.

Pilgrim Practicalities

The *Credencial* or "**pilgrim passport**" is a document carried by Camino walkers that allows access to pilgrim lodging and also bestows free or reduced entry to some museums and cathedrals. Collect stamps (*sellos*) at accommodations and other landmarks, which serve as proof of completing the pilgrimage to receive a *Compostela*. The *Compostela* is a document of completion awarded to those who walk at least the last 100km to Santiago or complete the last 200km by bicycle or on horseback. Present your completed credencial at the pilgrim office in Santiago in order to get the Compostela, written in Latin and personalized with your name and date of completion. Be sure to collect at least two stamps per day for the last 100km. Cardboard tubes are available for carrying your Compostela back home.

When to Go & Trip Length ☺

While the Camino can be walked in any season, summer and autumn are generally considered the best times for the Inglés route.

- ⭐**Spring** - Cooler temperatures, flowers, most services open, rain likely
- ⭐**Summer** - Most popular and crowded, weather can be warm, all services open
- **Autumn** - Pleasant temperatures, most services open
- **Winter** - Cold and rainy with potential for snow, many services closed

How much time do I need? We recommend taking a week for the full itinerary to allow for 6 days walking and another day in Santiago. We have divided the journey into 6 daily stages, with average daily distance of 19km (11.8mi). Feel free to deviate from this pace, staying at intermediary accommodations, which are noted on maps and in the text.

Visas and Entry ◱

Spain is among the 26 Schengen states of the European Union (EU) that have no internal borders. Citizens of the USA, Canada, Australia, New Zealand, and some South American countries are issued a free visa upon arrival with valid passport, limited to 90 days within a 180-day period. Most African, Asian, Middle Eastern, and some South American nationalities must apply for an advance visa. Check EU regulations to see if your nationality requires an advance visa. ⚠ Check for relevant travel updates at **caminoguidebook.com** ◱.

Sleeping A H A ⌂ ◱

One of the unique features of the Camino routes is the network of affordable pilgrim lodging known as *albergues.* Albergues are simple **dormitory accommodations** intended for non-motorized pilgrims (traveling on foot, by bicycle or on horse). They are generally operated by the local municipality, parish, pilgrim confraternity, or a private owner. Many operate on a first-come first-serve basis, though most private albergues accept reservations. Lower-cost albergues often fill up quite early in the day during popular seasons. In particular, the albergue in Hospital de Bruma often fills quickly in the summer months. Most public albergues on the Camino Inglés are operated by the Xunta (governing body of Galicia) and have a standardized price of €8. They tend to be basic, and kitchens often lack cookware.

Costs typically range between €5-15 per person, with a few on a donation basis (*donativo*). Amenities range from very basic to all the "bells and whistles" like wifi, washer, dryer, guest kitchen, etc. Amenities are shown in the text through symbols (legend on inside back cover). Accommodations with their own website have a ◱ symbol (links listed at **caminoguidebook.com**). Unless otherwise noted, assume that all albergues offer a mattress, pillow, bathroom with shower, and a place to handwash clothing. It's expected that you will bring a sleeping bag or sleep sack. The person in charge of an albergue is called a *hospitalero* (male) or *hospitalera* (female), and is often a volunteer. In areas with fewer dedicated pilgrim services, **hotels** and **pensions** often offer special pilgrim prices.

Spain offers a wide range of accommodations, from simple rooms with shared bathrooms in family-run pensions to opulent hotels. **A Hostel/Albergue** prices refer to a dormitory bed. If a hostel also has **A H private rooms**, the prices indicate dorm bed/single room/double room prices (€10/30/50). For **H hotels**, we list the single (if available)/double prices per room. Most albergues are open from around April 1 to November 1, with some staying open year round. Note that hotel prices are significantly higher in July/Aug. There are a few formal **A campgrounds** on the route, but carrying a tent is uncommon as "wild camping" is not generally permitted, and reasonably priced lodging is available each night.

Eating

Cafes and restaurants are not as readily available as on the Francés route. We list town and villages with restaurants, but in smaller towns the open hours can vary. Larger towns and cities have grocery stores, and it is wise to carry some snacks. Dinner often consists of a *Menú Peregrino* with starter, main dish, wine, bread and dessert for around €10-15. Some lodging have a guest kitchen where you can cook your own meal. With special dietary considerations, such as gluten free, vegetarian or vegan, it may be challenging to find food that fits your needs in restaurants, especially since meat and animal products are staples of Spanish cuisine. Grocery stores in cities typically have a wide variety of foods including gluten-free products, so plan ahead and carry some extra supplies.

Transportation

The closest airports to to Ferrol are in A Coruña (40-60 min) and Santiago de Compostela (90 min). Common connecting cities are Madrid, Barcelona, London, and Paris. Some of the cities on the Inglés route are along the Renfe FEVE narrow gauge **railway line**, while most are on or near **bus lines**. Local buses service many smaller towns, but with unpredictable schedules and infrequent service. The simplest way to skip a small section is by taxi. Hitchhikers are rarely picked up and should assume all known risks. Towns and cities with daily transport access are labeled with respective symbols in stage chapters.

Money, Costs and Budgeting

The unit of **currency** in Spain is the euro, made up of 100 euro cents. The best way to obtain euros is to use ATM/cash machines, available in cities and many towns marked in text with ⊖ symbol. Pilgrim hostels and small town amenities work on a cash basis, but some hotels, restaurants, and shops accept credit cards. **Daily costs** for many pilgrims are simply lodging, food/drink and sometimes incidentals like first aid supplies, laundromat or luggage transfer. An average daily budget probably falls in the €30-50 range, depending on your frugality, though it may be possible to spend a bit less and definitely to spend a lot more, particularly if you prefer hotels to hostels. Currency: EU €1 ≈ USD $1.00 ≈ GBP £0.87 ≈ CAD $1.33

Bed Bugs ☑, a blood-sucking parasitic insect, are on the rise around the world and can be a minor problem along the Camino. While bed bugs do not carry any known diseases, bites can be very uncomfortable and cause painful rashes for some people, and they are very difficult to get rid of once infested. You can pretreat your sleeping bag and backpack with permethrin and check that any albergue you stay in has been fumigated recently to lower your chances of being bitten.

Phones and Internet ☎︎📶📱

You can enable international roaming on your home mobile phone plan or purchase a Spanish SIM card (which requires an unlocked phone). International roaming on many US and Canada based plans can be quite expensive, but is a good solution if only used for emergencies. T-Mobile has free international data and text on some US plans. Calling and messaging apps like WhatsApp, Viber or Skype can be used when you have a wifi connection if you choose not to have cellular data coverage.

> To call Spain (+34) from the USA: 011 - 34 - XXX-XXXX
>
> To call the USA and Canada (+1) from abroad: 00 - 1 - XXX-XXX-XXXX

Wifi 📶 ("wee-fee") is increasingly available along the route; many accommodations and cafés offer free access.

Luggage Transfer and Tours 📱

The Post Office (Correos) provides luggage transfer from Ferrol to Santiago for a flat fee of €20. Weight (<20kg) and distance (<25km/90km on bike) restrictions apply. Book online 📱, or call or WhatsApp ☎︎+34683440022. Note that often public albergues don't accept walkers who use transfer services.

Medical Care ✚

Spain has good medical care that is free for citizens and countries with reciprocal agreements. Citizens of Great Britain, Ireland and the EU need a European Health Insurance Certificate (EHIC). Non-EU citizens are recommended to have private health and travel insurance. Carry an emergency contact card with known allergies, pertinent medical history, and information that is helpful to medical staff if you are unable to communicate. In emergencies, dial ☎︎112 to reach emergency services. Pharmacies are well stocked and readily available in cities and larger towns. 📱

Safety Issues

Spain has very low crime rates, and violent crime is extremely rare. It is always good to remain aware of your surroundings, not leave valuables unattended, and report any incidents to the police by dialing ☎︎112. Be extremely careful when walking along roads– always walk on the left side opposite traffic and remain alert. Try to avoid walking after dark. Aggressive **dogs** are not common but may be encountered. Carrying a walking stick can enhance confidence when encountering animals. All dogs in Spain are required to be vaccinated against rabies.

Additional planning information is available online at **caminoguidebook.com**, ☎ **caminocyclist.com**, and the Facebook group **Bikepacking the Camino** 📱

Packing for the Road: Gear, Resupply and Navigation
He who would travel happily must travel light. -Antoine de Saint-Exupéry

A light load makes for a happy pilgrim, and weight should be a primary concern in packing. A popular guideline is to pack no more than 10% of your body weight. Resist the temptation to pack many extras "just in case." Shops are readily available in Spain and most anything lacking can be purchased along the way.

Backpacks: A 30-40L (1800-2500in³) pack is sufficient for warm weather (40-60L for winter). Measure your torso length and choose a pack of the proper size, preferably being fitted at a knowledgeable outdoor retail store. Aim for a pack that weighs less than 1.4kg (3lbs) when empty.

Footwear: Light boots or sturdy trail runners with a stiff or semi-rigid sole offer protection for your feet and ankles against the often hard-surfaced, rocky and uneven path (trail surfaces, p. 12). Get fitted for footwear in the afternoon or evening after feet have expanded during the day. Bring some kind of lightweight footwear to wear in the evenings, such as flip-flops or foam sandals. ⚠ Be sure to thoroughly break in your footwear before beginning the Camino with practice hikes wearing your loaded pack. Invest in wool socks (not cotton), which wick moisture away from your skin, dry quickly, insulate when wet and manage odor better. If you're prone to blisters, experiment with liner socks (wool or polypropylene) to create an extra rubbing layer other than your skin.

Sleeping Bags: Most pilgrims prefer a lightweight, mummy-style, 1-season summer sleeping bag (rated ⁺40+°F/⁺5+°C) for the summer season. Some opt for only a sleeping bag liner in the heat of summer. For winter and the cool edges of fall and spring, it's a good idea to have a 3-season sleeping bag (rated ⁺15-⁺35°F/⁻10-0°C. Buy the lightest bag you can afford within your desired temperature range.

Clothing: Consider hiking clothes as layers, with inner layers for moisture management, middle for insulation, and outer for weather protection. The general rule for outdoor clothing is to avoid cotton as it does not retain insulating properties when wet and dries slowly. Synthetic materials (polyester, nylon, spandex) and wool (especially merino) are preferred, especially in cold and wet weather. In warm seasons, choose lightweight breathable clothes that provide sun protection.

Be prepared for the sun with a wide-brimmed **hat** and **sunglasses,** and use **sunscreen** regularly. Bring a **lightweight rain jacket** with a waterproof breathable membrane, or use a poncho that can also cover your backpack. Bring a waterproof pack cover or line your pack with plastic garbage bags to keep your gear dry. Pack electronics in zippered plastic bags or dry bags to protect against moisture.

Hypothermia is possible in wet, cool weather (as is common on the Inglés route), so be prepared with a dry set of clothes (socks included) for after a rainy day and bring one insulating layer, such as a warm fleece or down sweater.

Water and refills: While water is readily available most days of the Camino, it is important to carry sufficient amounts. Always carry at least one liter, and refill often. Carry more than two liters on hot days or in more remote areas. Reliable water refill sites are marked on stage maps (🚰). Tap water in Spain is treated and drinkable (*potable*). Most historic springs are marked as undrinkable (*no potable*) because they have not been treated or tested. Bottled water is widely available, but less environmentally-friendly than refillable bottles.

Dehydration and heat-related illness: Dehydration can lead to fatigue, headaches, heat exhaustion and heat stroke (a dangerous and life-threatening condition). Be sure to eat foods that help to replenish electrolytes and consider an electrolyte drink, such as Aquarius™, on hot days. If you become dehydrated and overheated and are unable to cool down, take a break in a cool, shady place, rehydrate with electrolytes and cool with a wet cloth or fanning until you feel better.

Fitness and Training: The Camino is not a technically challenging hike, but the journey's length and hard surfaces day after day takes a toll on the body. Taking the time to practice before beginning the pilgrimage will greatly reduce possible injuries. Training walks will help you get used to your gear, the weight on your feet and shoulders, and any other potential issues you might be able to prevent. It's wise to get used to full-day walks, taking 2-3 shorter walks per week and one full-day walk weekly with your loaded backpack. Check with your doctor if you have concerns about your health or fitness level, and start out slow and gradual.

Blister Prevention: The most common injury can cause an end to your trip.
- <u>At home</u>: choose properly fitting footwear. Try on many options before buying (foot should not move or slip when walking on various terrain types and grades). Use wool socks and liners. Break in footwear by taking hikes with a loaded pack prior to beginning the Camino.
- <u>On the trail</u>: keep feet cool and dry, take off shoes and socks for breaks, wash feet and socks daily, use liner socks.

Blister Treatment

- Take a break, remove socks to let feet cool and dry out. Check for hot spots and address by applying moleskin, Compeed®, or duct tape to create an additional rubbing surface to protect the hot spot.
- If a blister forms, use a sterilized needle to puncture its edge near the skin and drain using sterile materials. Air dry and re-dress blister with sterile bandages.
- If the blister or surrounding area becomes infected over the course of several days (increasing red appearance, tenderness, pus, red streaks), see a doctor.

For **dry or cracked feet** from primarily wearing sandals, consider wearing socks all the time to keep moisture in for cracks to heal.   **Impact-related injuries** are common with the large amount of paved surfaces on the Camino. If your feet and joints are taking a pounding, consider reducing your daily distance, walking on the softer shoulder near the paved path or adding walking poles and/or thicker socks.

The Trail: The paths that make up the Camino de Santiago covered in this book cover roughly 150km (93 miles) and vary greatly in trail surface, grade, landscapes, ecosystem, and climate. The Camino has more paved surfaces than many hikers expect, including sections of cobblestone, contributing to stress on feet and joints. 🅿 Paved / 🆄 Unpaved designations in this book refer to most obvious walking surface. There may be unpaved shoulders or footpaths along paved roads.

Route Finding, Trail Markings, Maps and GPS →
The Camino Inglés is generally well-marked, with a few sections where marks are more scarce and faded. The most common waymarks are painted yellow arrows (*flechas amarillas*) →, though a variety of other markings exist in different regions that incorporate yellow arrows or scallops shells into posts or signs. The most difficult sections to navigate are through large cities, where routes are often poorly marked and Camino markers compete with other signs. For this reason, we've included a number of detailed city maps throughout this book, though note that the maps are representative and not exhaustive, without every street name. When there is more than one marked route option, we provide a brief overview of both options and show them numbered on the map. **GPS/smart phone route files are on our website, as well as tips for use.** 🗗

The path is well marked with yellow arrows.

Daily Stages and Regional Sections: This book organizes the Camino Inglés into 6 daily stages from Ferrol (4 from A Coruña) averaging about 19km (11.8 miles)per day. The page spreads introducing each stage include a stage map, elevation profile, total distance, total ascent and descent in meters (▲/▼), paved/unpaved (🅿/🆄) percentages, difficulty level (see below), time estimate (☺), and a list of towns with albergues/pilgrim lodging.

Stages begin and end at the main or largest albergue in the beginning and ending locality whenever possible. For mid-stage towns and points of interest without albergues, measurements are taken from the town center or main church, whichever is prominent or closest to the marked route. Cumulative stage distances are noted on the stage maps and correspond to distances listed in town listings and elevation charts. Distances for off-route accommodations or points of interest are indicated with a plus symbol (example: +1.3km). Towns list resources available, all the albergues, and a selection of private accommodations in varying price ranges.

Distances are measured in metric units (kilometers and meters), and elevation in meters (m). In **elevation tables,** note that y-axis intervals vary, and relative scales are indicated with color-coded arrows ↕↕↕, which may not correspond to the stage's difficulty rating color. ☺ Estimated **walking time** for each stage assumes a pace of 3-5 km/hour (1.8-3 mph) with terrain and elevation considered. Factor extra time for breaks and exploration.

Each day's stage route is assigned a **difficulty level** from 1-3. These ratings consider an "average" walker, who is reasonably fit but not necessarily athletic or an experienced hiker. A "Challenging" stage will likely have some characteristics listed below. Exercise caution in colder months (Nov-Mar) when snow, cold rain and hypothermia a greater possibility.

Length:
1m = 1yd or 3ft
100m ≈ 100yd
1km = 0.62 miles
10km = 6.2 miles
1.6km = 1 mile

▭▭▭ **Easy:** Slight elevation change, sturdy footing, water easily accessible
▭▭▭ **Moderate:** More elevation change, steeper grades, longer distance, some challenging terrain
▭■■ **Challenging:** Significant elevation change, longer distances, some sections of rocky/loose/narrow paths with less stable footing, water sources may be scarce, trail is more remote and exposed (fewer shelter and services nearby in case of bad weather or emergencies)

This **map guidebook** is designed to be lightweight and minimalist. It provides detailed stage and city maps, pilgrim lodging as well as select hotels, listing of amenities in relevant towns and cities, and basic preparation, background information, and tips ☀ when helpful. Visit **caminoguidebook.com** for expanded planning information. ⎘

Packing List ☞

HIKING GEAR ESSENTIALS

- ☐ **Backpack** (30-40L)
- ☐ **Sleeping bag or bag liner**, lightweight
- ☐ **Navigation**: guidebook, GPS (optional)
- ☐ **Headlamp** or flashlight/torch
- ☐ **Sun protection**: hat, sunglasses, sunscreen and lip balm
- ☐ **Towel**, lightweight travel type
- ☐ **Water bottles** and/or **hydration system** (2L)
- ☐ **Waterproof pack cover/poncho**
- ☐ **Pocket/utility knife** (checked luggage)
- ☐ **Lighter** or **matches** (buy locally)
- ☐ **Toiletries** (list opposite)
- ☐ **Personal items** (list opposite)
- ☐ **First aid kit** (list opposite)

Take the time to visit a quality outdoor gear shop to get fitted for a backpack that is comfortable and footwear that fits properly.

FOOTWEAR & CLOTHING

- ☐ **Footwear** (boots or trail runners)
- ☐ **Sandals** or flip-flops
- ☐ **Hiking socks** (3 pairs wool)
- ☐ **Sock liners** (1-2 pairs wicking)
- ☐ **Pants** (1-2 pairs quick-drying, zip-offs, or shorts)
- ☐ **Short-sleeved shirts**, tank tops (
- ☐ **Long-sleeved shirts** (1-2)
- ☐ **Light fleece** or jacket
- ☐ **Waterproof jacket** or poncho
- ☐ **Underwear** (3 pairs)
- ☐ **Sports bras** (2)
- ☐ **Bandana** or Buff
- ☐ **Swimsuit** (optional)
- ☐ **Warm hat***
- ☐ **Insulating jacket***
- ☐ **Long underwear** top/bottom*

*only necessary in cold s

ADDITIONAL GEAR (OPTIONAL)

- ☐ **Hiking poles**: Used correctly, poles can take up to 25% pressure off of your leg joints. Poles are great for stability, especially going up and down hills, and serve double-duty as a means to chase away dogs. Worthwhile for anyone with joint issues. Inexpensive poles can be purchased in on
- ☐ **Sleeping mat**: A lightweight foam pad can come in handy for sitting on and for sleeping if albe are full or have limited beds. You can often find left behind mats for free along the Camino.
- ☐ **Pillowcase**: Most albergues have pillows but do not change the pillowcases regularly, a spare T-s can also be stretched over the pillow as a makeshift case.
- ☐ **Stuff sacks** or cloth bags with drawstrings don't weigh much and keep you organized
- ☐ **Reusable nylon grocery bag**: Comes in handy as a laundry bag, purse and grocery bag
- ☐ **Clothespins** or safety pins for hanging laundry.
- ☐ **Travel cooking pot and utensils**: Many of the albergues in Galicia have kitchens, but no kitche equipment whatsoever. If you are intent on cooking your own dinners, you may wish to bring a lightweight cooking pot, or purchase one when you arrive in Galicia.
- ☐ **Camping gear:** Lightweight tent (TarpTent) or bivy sack, camping stove, a pot and utensils, and extra water carrying capacity. (See Camping p. 7).

*For recommendations on specific brands and models, visit **caminoguidebook.com**. ☞

*Decathlon is a chain of outdoor gear retailers throughout Spain a store in Santiago de Compostel as well as Madrid and Barcelona. ☞

COILETRIES

Don't pack too much. Bring small refillable travel bottles of shampoo and conditioner <100mL/4oz. Refill from items left behind (ask at the albergues) or buy your own refill and share.

❏ **Shampoo/conditioner** (100mL/4oz bottles)
❏ **Toothbrush** and **toothpaste** (travel sized)
❏ **Soap**, biodegradable bar or liquid, such as Dr. Bronner's™
❏ **Laundry detergent** (powder works well and weighs less) or 100mL/4 oz. bottle or solid bar
❏ **Toilet paper** or tissues (albergues frequently run out)
❏ **Deodorant** (optional, you will stink with or without it!)
❏ **Hand sanitizer** (optional)
❏ **Contact solution** (if necessary), replace at pharmacies

FIRST AID/MEDICAL KIT

Supplies are available in pharmacies along the route and most albergues have a basic medical kit. It's always best to be prepared with at least a few day's worth of each supply. Keep it light!

❏ Any **prescription medicine** you need
❏ Variety of **Band-Aids®/plasters, sterile gauze pads**
❏ Antiseptic towelettes or **wound disinfectant**
❏ **Antibiotic ointment**
❏ **Medical tape**
❏ **Elastic bandage** (such as ACE™)
❏ **Pain reliever/fever reducer** (such as acetaminophen or ibuprofen)
❏ **Antihistamine** (such as Benadryl®)
❏ **Anti-diarrheal** medicine: loperamide hydrochloride (Imodium®)
❏ **Blister treatment** (such as Moleskin or Compeed®)
❏ **Safety pins**
❏ **Baby powder** (helps with chafing)
❏ Small **scissors** and **tweezers**

PERSONAL ITEMS (OPTIONAL)

❏ **Travel wallet**: with passport/ID, health insurance card, pilgrim passport, money, credit cards, ATM card, etc. Stash an extra ATM card or wad of cash somewhere separate from your wallet.
❏ **Earplugs**: high quality noise-canceling earplugs are essential for a good night's sleep.
❏ **Mobile phone** and **charger** (see Phones and Internet p. 9)
❏ **Camera, charger, memory cards**, compact USB flash drive for backup
❏ **Journal with pen/pencil**: highly recommended for remembering the details of each day, reflecting more fully on the experience and recording contact info of new friends.
❏ **Tablet or e-reader:** useful for checking email and for pleasure reading without carrying heavy books. Photos of family and home are good conversation starters.
❏ **Book** for pleasure reading (just bring one and trade when you're done)
❏ **Plug/currency converter** for any electrical appliances (European plugs run on 220V with two round prongs. Most electronics run on 110-220V, labeled on device, requiring only a plug converter and not a currency converter.)
❏ **Zippered plastic bags or waterproof stuff sacks** for keeping electronics and other valuables dry and organized.
❏ **Pilgrim's shell**

FERROL TO NEDA

14.4km (9.0mi), ▲ 305ᴍ / ▼ 310ᴍ, ☉ 3.5-5 Hᴏᴜʀs
🅿 62%, 8.9km / Ⓤ 38%, 5.5km, Dɪꜰꜰɪᴄᴜʟᴛʏ: ▬◻◻

Approaching Neda along the Ría de Ferrol

☀ Start from Ferrol's pilgrim office at the Porto de Curuxeiras and continue through the city center. Take a moment to enjoy the views of the city's port from the overlook by the Ferrol Parador hotel. Return toward the sea, passing several naval training bases, before reaching Praia de Caranza and enjoying coastal views walking to Xubia and then on to Neda.

0.0 Ferrol 🅗🅘🍴🚉🛏⊕✚€🅘🔲🚻 See map and accommodations on p. 16-17.
Ferrol has long been a naval center and important port, as well as home to major shipbuilding yards. Ferrol was the birthplace of Spanish dictator and *caudillo* (strongman) Francisco Franco. From 1939-1982, the city was officially known as El Ferrol del Caudillo.

ⓘ The **tourist info office** at the Porto de Curuxeiras offers helpful information on navigation (city maps and Camino Inglés brochures available) and sightseeing in Ferrol (☉Tues-Fri 10am-1pm, 4-6pm; Sat-Sun, holidays 10am-2pm, 4-6pm; Mon closed).

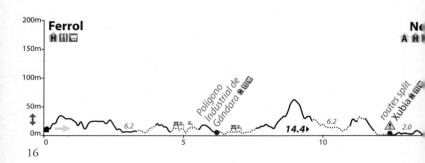

0.0 Ferrol 🏨🍴🛒🛏️⊙⊕€🛈🅿️♿

1. **🏨 Parador de Ferrol** (€75+ 🛏️): 🍴🛜, Praza do Contralmirante Azarola Gresillón, 📞981356720 📱, pilgrim discounts
2. **🏨 El Suizo** (€49-54/56-62): 🆆🅳🛜⊙, Dolores 67, 📞981300400 📱
3. **🏨 Hostal El Cairo** (€22+/35+): 🆆🅳🛜⊙, Dolores 32, 📞981353266 📱
4. **🏨 Hotel Real** (€35/50): 🛜⊙, Dolores 11-13, 📞981351586 📱
5. **🏨 Hotel Almendra** (€38-47/45-55): 🍴🆆🅳🛜⊙, Almendra, 📞981358190 📱
6. **🏨 Pensión La Parra** (€15/25): 🛜⊙, Carmen 19, 📞606599333
7. **🏨 Hostal Zahara** (€22+/33+): 🍴🛜⊙, Pardo Bajo 28, 📞981351231 📱
8. **🏨 Hostal La Frontera** (€18+/26+): 🍴🆆🅳🛜⊙, San Andrés 4, 📞881953036 📱
9. **🏨 Choyo 2** (€17/34): 🍴🛜, Carlos III 67, 📞981948908 📱
10. **🏨 Gran Hotel** (€43+/53+): 🍴🛜, Castilla 75, 📞981330226 📱
11. **🏨 América** (€30-45/39-50): 🍴🛜⊙, Sánchez Calviño 70-76, 📞981370208 📱
12. **🏨 Silva** (€29/36+): 🍴🛜⊙, Rio Castro 42, 📞981310552 📱
13. **🏨 Valencia** (€36+/40+ 🛏️): 🍴🛜⊙, Catabois 390, 📞981370352
14. **🏨 Casa Juanito** (€19+/30+): 🍴🛜⊙, Concepción Arenal 163, 📞981388454 📱
15. **🏨 Odeón** (€45): 🍴🆆🛜⊙🛏️, Cataluña 20, 📞981372951 📱, Polígono Gándara

9.3 San Martín Monastery

Records of the San Martín (San Martiño) Monastery date to 977, while the current building was constructed in the 12th century in Romanesque style.

12.4 Xubia 🏨🍴🛒➕🛏️♿

Shortly after crossing a wide river/estuary, the route splits on the edge of Xubia when you reach a T intersection with a paved bike/pedestrian path (12.4km). Turn L to enter Xubia, or take the pedestrian way R, following the river to a walking bridge to cross the river and arrive at the Neda albergue.

🏨 Marcial (€25/35): 🍴🛜⊙, Río Pereiro 5, 📞981384417 📱

🏨 Kensington (€25/35): 🍴🛜⊙, Castilla 832, 📞981387326 📱

14.4 Neda 🅰️🏨🍴🛒➕⊙🛏️♿

Most lodging and services are located on the northern edge of Neda. The town center and other private accommodations are several kilometers south of the albergue. The Iglesia de San Nicolás is 2.2km south of the albergue, just off route as you pass Mesón O Recuncho. Originally built in the 14th century in Gothic style, later 18th and 19th century renovations produced a Baroque facade.

1. **🅰️ Xunta** (🛏️28, €8): 🍳🆆🛜⊙, O Empedrón, 📞682623335/981390233, ⊙all year, if locked, check the door for instruction
2. **🏨 Pensión Maragoto** (€15-27/29-40): 🍴🛜⊙, Xubia 12, 📞981347538/658488074 📱 nice café/restaurant with pilgrim menu
3. **🏨 Pazo da Merced** (€90+ 🛏️): 🍴🛜⊙🛏️, Pazo da Merced, 📞981382200 📱, <u>3km past Neda, +400m</u>, see stage 2 map for location

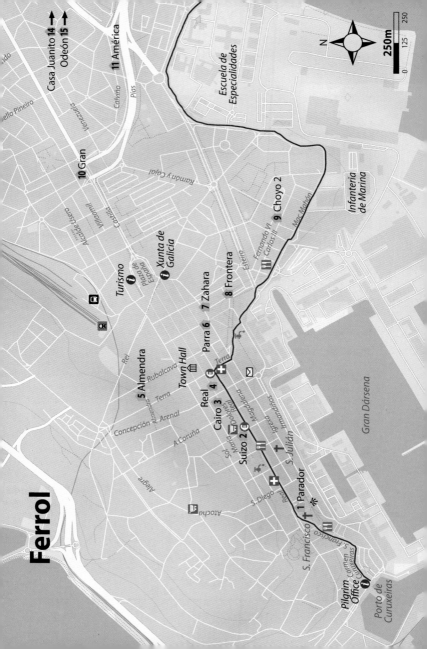

Ferrol

Casa Juanito 14
Odeón 15
11 América
10 Gran

Escuela de Especialidades

Infantería de Marina

Alcalde Usero
Villaamil
Calviño
Pías
Venezuela
Castilla
Ramón y Cajal

Turismo
Plaza de España
Xunta de Galicia

9 Choyo 2
Fernando VI
Carlos III
Mac Mahón

8 Frontera
Esteiro

7 Zahara
6 Parra
Rei
Rubalcava
Terra
Almira
Concepción
Arenal
A Coruña
Terra
Town Hall
5 Almendra
4 Real
3 Cairo
Sol
Sta. María
Dolores
Real
Magdalena
Terra
2 Suizo
Irmandiños
Pardiñas
S. Diego
Real
S. Jullán
1 Parador

Gran Dársena

Alegre
Atocha
Carmen
S. Francisco
Curuxeiras

Pilgrim Office

Porto de Curuxeiras

N

250m
0 125 250

2 NEDA TO PONTEDEUME

15.0km (9.4mi), ▲ **467m** / ▼ **485m**, **4-5 Hours**

P 87%, 13.1km / U 13%, 1.9km, **Difficulty:**

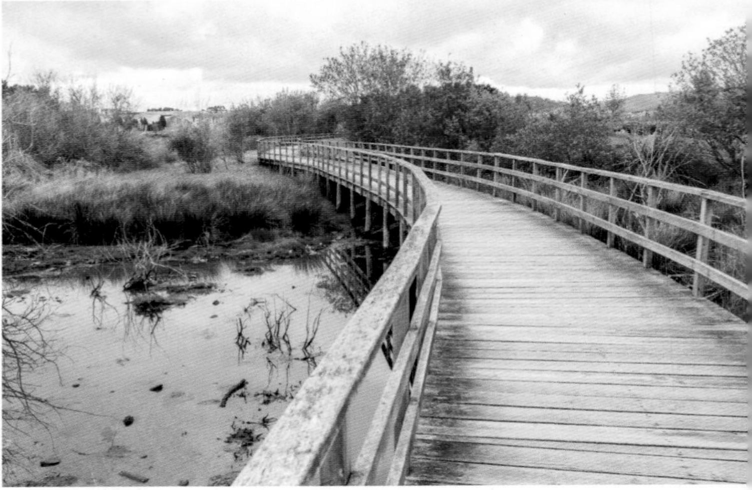

Boardwalk shortly after leaving the Neda albergue

Walk south along the Ría de Ferrol, then pass through Neda's lovely historic cente Continue inland, passing through Fene and ascending through several small villages on tl way to the historic city of Pontedeume, named for its bridge over the Río Eume.

5.8 **Fene** H

Lodging and train station are significantly off-route.

H **Pensión A Cepa** (€25/35-40): , Hortela 16, 981341352, +1.2km off-route in Perlio (across from Perlio train station)

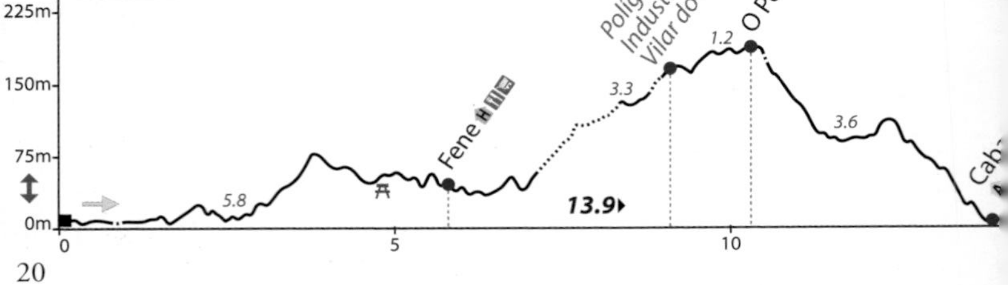

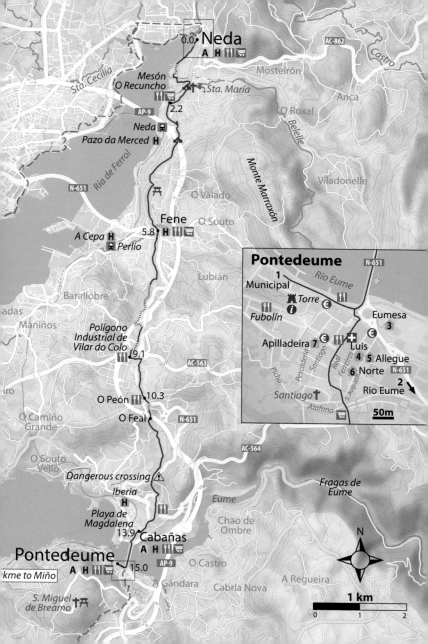

Neda
0.0
A H ⋔ 🛒

AC-862

Castro

Mosteirón

Mesón
O Recuncho
⋔

Sta. Cecilia

Sta. María

Anca

AP-9

O Roxal

2.2

Belelle

Neda 🚉
Pazo da Merced H

O Valado

Viladonelle

Ría de Ferrol

Monte Marraxón

N-651

⋔

O Souto

Fene
5.8   H ⋔ 🛒

A Cepa H
⚒ *Perlio*

Lubián

Barallobre

Maniños

Polígono
Industrial de
Vilar do Colo
⋔   9.1

AC-563

O Peón   10.3
O Feal   N-651

AC-564

Eume

Fragas de
Eume

Dangerous crossing ⚠

Iberia
H
Playa de
Magdalena   ⋔
13.9   **Cabañas**
A H ⋔ 🛒
AP-9   O Castro

Chao de
Ombre

Pontedeume
kme to Miño   A H ⋔   15.0

O Camiño
Grande

O Souto
Vello

S. Miguel
de Breamo   ✝ ⛺

O Gándara

A Regueira

Cabría Nova

N ↑

1 km

0   1   2

Pontedeume   N-651

1   *Río Eume*

Municipal
⋔ **Torre**   €
Fubolín ⋔   ℹ

Eumesa
3   €

Apilladeira 7   €   ⋔   ✚
Santiago   **Luis**
4 5 **Allegue**
6 **Norte**   N-651
Santiago ✝   2 **Río Eume** ↘

Atafona 🛒

50m

13.9 **Cabañas** A H 🍴 🛏 ➕ 🚌 ⛲   Galician: Cabanas/Praia da Magdalena

At the traffic circle just before the bridge into Pontedeume, turn right if you want to detour to the beach at Playa de Magdalena.

A Casa de Acogida San José (💤30, don): 📷, Palacio 11, 📞660244324/681171844, 🕐all year, +250m off-route, religious character, group-oriented but welcoming, call ahead

H Hotel Sarga (€60/80): 📶 ▦, Arenal 7, 📞981431000 ✉️

H Hotel Iberia (€33+/44+): 🍴 ▦ Ⓓ 📶 ⊙, Hilarioruiz 19, 📞981430749 ✉️, +1.1km

15.0 **Pontedeume** A H 🍴 🛒 ⊙ ➕ 🚫 ℹ️ 🚌 ⛲

1. **A Municipal** (💤20, €6): ⊙, Peirao, 📞659789716, phone numbers and open hours vary (see sign on door); more info at ℹ️ tourism office (📞981430270), mixed reviews
2. **A Río Eume** (💤20, €15): ▦ Ⓓ 📶, Club Firrete 19, 📞604036109, 🕐all year
3. **H Eumesa** (€45/60): 🍴 📶 ⊙, Coruña, 📞981430901
4. **H ⭐ Pensión Luis** (€18/36): 🍴 📶 ⊙, San Agustín 12, 📞981430235/666547984 ✉️
5. **H Hostal Allegue** (€15-20/30-40): 🍴 📶 ⊙, Chafaris 1, 📞981430035 ✉️, 📶 in bar
6. **H Hospedaje Bar Norte** (€30-40): 🍴 📶, San Agustín 26, 📞981434527, mixed reviews
7. **H Pensión Casa Apilladeira** (€45-55 🛏): 📶, Pescadería 19, 📞638962554, nice renovated rooms, reception at Bar Fubolín

Pontedeume takes its name from the old stone bridge that crosses the Río Eume. The 850m bridge was the longest in Spain for many years and dates to the 14th century. (The current version was completed in the 19th century.)

The bridge from which Pontedeume draws its name

The Iglesia de Santiago is an 18th-century church built over a 16th-century church. Inside lies the 16th-century tomb of Fernando de Andrade. The powerful Andrade family, which emerged in the 12th century, commissioned much of the architecture in town, including the Pazo dos Condes (the Andrade family mansion). Now all that remains of the mansion is the impressive Torre de Andrade. Pontedeume's tourism office is now located in the bottom of the tower.

The *feirón* is a weekly market held every Saturday—mostly small stands with local foodstuffs, and the ♦ Festa das Peras (Pear Festival) takes place on the first Sunday in September, honoring the Virgin of As Virtudes and San Nicolás de Tolentino.

Several kilometers outside of town, the Fragas do Eume Natural Park consists of one of the last remaining old-growth Atlantic forests in Europe. Also outside of town, the 12-century Romanesque Iglesia de San Miguel de Breamo sits atop Monte de Breamo (305m) with views of the surrounding area. Pontedeume's residents make pilgrimages to the church on May 8 and September 29; if you have time, the site is worth a detour (+3.0km).

If this day feels short, you prefer ending your day by the beach, or you just want to stay somewhere other than Pontedeume's less-than-stellar municipal albergue, consider continuing 10km to Miño, a pleasant seaside town with a simple but nice Xunta albergue. From Miño, you can walk a very short day (~10km) to Betanzos or a longer day (22.4km) to Presedo (in the process shortening the following day's walk to Hospital de Bruma).

Pontedeume's harbor on the Río Eume

PONTEDEUME TO BETANZOS

20.2km (12.6mi), ▲ **884M** / ▼ **862M**, ⊙ **5-7 HOURS**

🅟 75%, 15.1km / 🅤 25%, 5.1km, **DIFFICULTY:** ▭▬▯

Views of the Betanzos Estuary

☀ Climb steeply out of Pontedeume and enjoy several kilometers of enjoyable walking through rural countryside. If you're lucky enough to walk in the spring, enjoy colorful fields of roadside flowers. Descend to Miño, detouring to the sandy beach at Praia Grande if you wish. Leave Miño and follow the Río Lambre before crossing an old stone bridge. On the other side of the Lambre, ascend through a number of small villages and descend once again to Betanzos, a lovely town full of history and beautiful architecture.

1.2 Campolongo 🛏🍴➕, +275m

Town is +275m on N-651, shortly after passing the turnoff for San Miguel de Breamo.
🛏 **Pensión Mesón Paz** (€20/30-40): 🍴🛜◎, Campo Longo 92, ☎981432024 ⤴

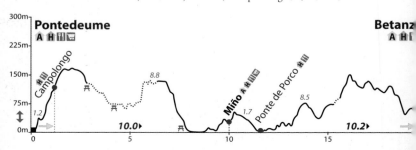

Pontedeume 0.0

A H ⫠⫪ 🏠

AP-9

Vizús

O Castro

Eume

A Gándara

Cabría Nova

S. Miguel de Breamo ✝⛩ 1.2

Campolongo

H ⫪ +275m

Ver

Sambollo

⛩ Buíña

Campolong-Cruceiro

Boebre

Bollo

Ría de Betanzos

CP-4803

⛩

O Fondal

Costa Miño

N-651

Morteirado

Bañobre

⛩

Leiro

Baxoi

22.4km from Miño to Presedo

Miño

A H ⫪ 🛒 10.0

A Folgueira

O Chao

Praia da Alameda

A Ponte de Porco

H ⫪

11.7

de Gardario Moruxo

AC-162

A Ponte de Lambre

Lambre

AC-164

Trasmil

Lambre

arrio

15.6 Chantada

Sas H

O Tercio

Covas

AP-9

🕸

Gas

O Castro de S. Fiz

N-651

✝ S. Martiño

N

Caraña de Arriba

Paderme

Mandeo

2 km
1   2

🚉

20.2

✝ N.S. do Camiño

Betanzos

A H ⫪ 🛒 🏠

Meñdo

Mandeo

Miño (inset)

Praia Grande

⫪

🛒

Xunta **1**

🚉 ➕ ➕

ℹ️

🛒 ✉️

🛒 €

2 Terraza

Miño

200m

Betanzos (inset)

✝ S. Francisco

✝ Sta. Maria

Pescadería

Casa da Pescadería **1**

2 Santa Maria

Torre de Reloxo

🛒

Nova

➕

€

Betanzos

⫪

Praza Alfonso IX

✉️

Garelos **4**

ℹ️

Rollo

Venezuela

✝ Sto. Domingo

🕸

Río Mandeo

Hórreo **5**

🛒 **3**

Jesús García Naveira

N-651

Rosalía de Castro

Villa **6**

Castelao

100m

10.0 Miño A H ⊞⚖➕✚€𝒊▢▣

Most services are on route, but the albergue and the beach require a detour.

1. **A** Xunta (↳22, €8): 🏠🛜⊙, As Marismas, ☎607803569, ⊙1-10pm all year, clean, pleasant, close to beach +750m
2. **H** Hostal La Terraza (€28-33/35-55): 🛜⊙, Carreira 4, ☎657629292/617034492 📱, 🍽 breakfast included in summer

11.7 Ponte de Porco H ⊞

H Habitaciones Brisa (€40): ⊞🛜, ☎981782022

15.6 Sas H, +1.6km

H Casa de Sixto (€40-60/60-75): ⊞🅦🛜▤, Sas 44, ☎981782831/659468452 📱, +1.6km

20.2 Betanzos A H ⊞⚖⊙➕€𝒊▢▣

Betanzos is a beautiful historic town nestled on a hilltop at the mouth of the Betanzos Estuary between the Mandeo and Mendo Rivers. Originally a hill fort called Brigantium, today Betanzos has one of the best-preserved old quarters in Galicia.

1. **A** ☆ Casa da Pescadería (Xunta, ↳32, €8): 🏠🅦🄳🛜⊙, Pescadería 4, ☎616944470/618331787, ⊙1-10pm all year, nicely renovated in beautiful building
2. **A** Santa María del Azogue (↳16, €12): 🏠🅦🄳🛜, Santa María 1, ☎683193256/981819635, ⊙all year
3. **A** Río Mandeo (↳24, €17/-/70): 🏠🅦🄳⊙, Doctor Fleming 3, ☎604044448 📱, ⊙all year

Iglesia de San Francisco

4. **H Garelos** (€55+/66+ 🛏): 📶 ⊙, Alfonso IX 8, ☎981775930 ✉️
5. **H El Hórreo** (€15 per person): 📷 ⊙, Venezuela 26-28, ☎669191387
6. **H Villa de Betanzos** (€40-65/50-79): 🍴 📶 ⊙, Castilla 38, ☎981776682/638350002,
   call ahead if traveling by bike

The Iglesia de San Francisco was built in 1387 by order of Count Fernán Pérez de Andrade. His tomb, decorated with hunting motifs, is located inside the church complex. Not far away, the Iglesia de Santiago dates to the 15th century. The church's main door is decorated with a statue of St. James on horseback. The city center boasts a beautiful 16th-century clock tower, and much of the city is surrounded by its original medieval wall, in which three of the four original gates are preserved.

🎪 In July, Betanzos hosts a medieval festival, which recreates the hustle and bustle of a medieval market. In August, Betanzos celebrates the festival of San Roque by launching a large paper balloon. Betanzos is also famous for its tortilla española—don't miss it!

A pilgrim on dirt roads before Miño

BETANZOS TO BRUMA

24.8km (15.5mi), ▲ 1028m / ▼ 659m, ☉ 7-9 Hours
🅿 61%, 15.3km / Ⓤ 39%, 9.6km, **Difficulty:** ▬▬■■

Spring flowers along a dirt road before Cos

☼ Leave coastal towns behind and climb into beautiful rural Galician countryside on the way to Hospital de Bruma, a historic pilgrim rest stop and meeting point of the routes from A Coruña and Ferrol. The day's walk is more demanding than previous days, but the increasingly attractive scenery is worth the effort. Services are fewer and farther between than on previous days, so plan accordingly!

⚠ **Route Option**: The route splits in Cos for 3.6km. Pass the Iglesia San Esteban de Cos and continue to the main road (DP-0105). After 160m on DP-0105, the old Camino Inglés route (⭐ recommended and highlighted) goes R on a small residential paved road, while the new official route continues straight on DP-0105. ⚠ *The marks from the old route have been erased, so do not attempt it without a GPS track. This old route is a more appealing option as the main (official) route simply follows the main road.*

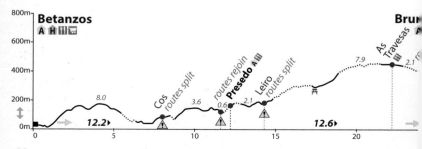

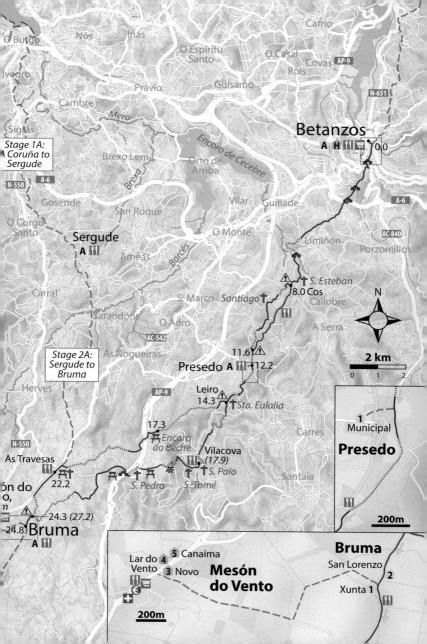

12.2 **Presedo** A 🍴

🍴 Restaurant Museu Xente is 550m south of the albergue (access via DP-0105 or Camino route). ⚠ This is the last food/water before Bar Casa Avelina in As Travesas (22.2km).
A **Municipal** (🛏16, €7): 🏧☀, Campo de La Saleta, 📞644035292,
  ☀all year, call phone # on door for entry; registration and payment at 7pm

⚠ **Route Option**: The route splits again in Leiro (14.3km) at a T intersection after Iglesia de Santa Eulalia. The new official route turns R then L and follows the main road (DP-0105) 300m before turning R onto a gravel road that ascends gradually to the Encoro do Beche (Beche Dam). The old route turns L at the T and continues on paved roads and dirt tracks through rural villages before making a steep ascent from Vilacova. Once again, the marks for the old route have been erased at the intersection but soon reappear past the intersection. The official route (recommended) is 2.9km shorter and has a more manageable grade, even if it does miss an occasional view and the lovely Bar Julia in Vilacova.

A cyclist on dirt tracks leading to Bruma

The Xunta albergue is housed in a restored historical pilgrim hospital.

24.8 Bruma A 🏠

The Xunta albergue is located in a former medieval pilgrim hostel (Hospital de Bruma). This interesting renovated building has limited beds (22), so try to get in early if you can. A cafe by the albergue has a daily menu and also serves breakfast. A food truck comes in the afternoons Wednesday to Saturday. If the albergue is full, there are several private accommodation options in Mesón do Vento (+1.7km), as well as restaurants and grocery stores.

1. **A Xunta** (🛏22, €8): 🎒⊙, ☎981687001/981692921, ⊙1-10pm all year, kitchen is quite limited (no utensils)
2. **A San Lorenzo de Bruma** (🛏22, €20/-/55): 🎒 W D 🛜, ☎619464240

24.8 Mesón do Vento 🏠🍴🛒➕⊙🔲, +1.7km

There are bus stops on N-550 across from the gas station and Hotel Canaima. Monbus operates a line that travels frequently between Santiago and A Coruña. Northbound buses to A Coruña stop on the east side of the road; southbound buses to Santiago stop on the west side of the road.

3. **H Mesón Novo Pensión** (€26-37/42-46): 🍴🛜⊙, Santiago Apóstol 86, ☎981692776/678585431 🖃, will pick up pilgrims who have reservation
4. **H Lar do Vento** (€70 for 4-person apartment): 🎒 W 🛜⊙, Santiago Apóstol 61, ☎683336918 🖃
5. **H Canaima** (€33+/52+): 🍴🛜⊙, Santiago Apóstol 67, ☎981692891 🖃, will pick up pilgrims who have reservation from 🍴 Casa Avelina in As Travesas or albergue in Bruma (until 6:30pm)

BRUMA TO SIGÜERO

24.5km (15.3mi), ▲ 412M / ▼ 574M, ⏱ 6-8 HOURS
🅿 65%, 16.0km / Ⓤ 35%, 8.5km, **DIFFICULTY:** ▬▬☐

The Camino continues on a forested dirt path after Carballo

💡 Head south from Bruma and amble along minor country roads. You pass little of note and are often on paved roads, but the walking through rural countryside is enjoyable. As you approach Sigüero, the final few kilometers follow a major highway—thankfully much of this section stays on dirt roads. When you leave the highway, pass an industrial park before reaching Sigüero.

While there are few on-route accommodation options, several towns not far from the official route (Castrelos, Ordes, and A Igrexa) have private room accommodations.

3.5 Castrelos Ⓗ🍴, +1.9km
Turn R and leave the official route after Café O Porto to reach Castrelos.
Ⓗ **Barreiro** (€30/50): 🍴Ⓦ◻🛜Ⓞ, N-550 KM32, ☎981680917 ☑

6.9 A Rúa Ⓗ🍴
Ⓗ **Casa Rural Dona María** (€57+/91+): 🔞🍴🛜Ⓞ, Lugar A Rúa 12, ☎675680108 ☑

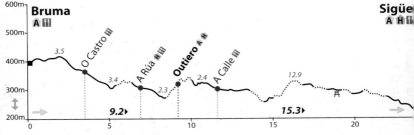

Mesón do Vento
(+1.7km)
H

A Brea

Bruma 0.0
A

Viris

A Lobo

Queixas

Vilasenín

Encoro de
Vilasenín

Mejtufe

Barcula

Visatoña

N-550

Perra

AP-9

Olás

O Castro 3.5

† S. Pedro

Castrelos, H
+1.9km

Lesta

As Mámoas

Cestaños

A Rúa 6.9
H

Ordes
(+2.6km)
H

O Pedrouzo

AC-524
Abellá

Castenda
de Parada

Outeiro
A H

9.2

O Empalme

Liste

Barbeiros

A Estación

A Calle 11.6

Samo

O Pazo

Paradela

Carballo 12.9

A Cruz de
Folgoso

O Carballal

Abongo

A Igrexa
(+2.0km)
H

Vilasuso

Castelo

Os Carballos
Fonte da
Santiña

N-550

Valverde

Berdomas

Tambre

A Torre

O Vilar

N

Polígono
Industrial

Sigüero 24.5
A H

km
1   2

Maruzo

Vilanova 5

N-550

Carbeiro

Sigüero

Camiño Real
2 Ultreia
et Suseia

1

4
Sigüero

3 Mirás

Tambre

100m

8.3 Ordes H ⓘ▦⊙➕⊜❒✺, +2.6km

1.4km past A Rúa, the Camino route turns L, leaving the larger paved road, continuing onto a gravel road, and crossing a stream. To go to Ordes, stay straight on the larger paved road.

H **Nogallás** (€30/45): ⓌⒹ🛜⊙, Alfonso Senra 110, ☎981680155 ⤢

9.2 Outeiro A H

A **Rectoral de Poulo** (Xunta, ⟷42, €8): 🔀⊙, 🕒all year

H **Antón Veiras** (€45-50/50-60 🛏): ⓘⓌⒹ🛜⊙, Outeiro de Abaixo 2, ☎981682303/686715005, just off route 200m after crossing under AC-524

15.0 A Igrexa H ⓘ, +2.0km

Cross a bridge over a stream 1.4km past Carballo, and continue on a small paved road. After 700m, the Camino route turns L onto a dirt road, leaving the paved road. To go to A Igrexa, continue on the paved road.

H **Santa Cruz** (€25/30-40): ⓘ🛜⊙, Lugar de Iglesia 36, ☎981681452 ⤢

Galician pastureland

24.5 **Sigüero** A H 🅷⬛🛒➕⊖⊡

1. **A H Camiño Real** (🛏22, €15-18/30-50 ⬛): 🏠⬛🅦🅓📶⊙, Ourense 9, ☎648746023/981691657/685110377 ☑, ⊙all year, clean, pleasant

2. **A Ultreia et Suseia** (🛏10, €15/-/40): 🅚⬛🅦🅓📶⊙, Campo 4, ☎638177894

3. **A Mirás** (🛏14, €15): 🅚�ⅱ🅦🅓📶⊙, Compostela 16, ☎881981909 ☑, ⊙1pm Feb-Oct

4. **H Sigüero Hostel** (€30-45/52-65 ⬛): �ⅱ🅦🅓📶⊙, Plaza Alexandre Bóveda 1, ☎981973636/615499071 ☑, nice terrace along stream

5. **H Pensión Vilanova** (€45-55 ⬛): 📶⊙, Alto de Vilanova Oroso, ☎630125544 ☑, positive reviews, +1.2km on N-550, cross to west side of AP-9 at north end of industrial park (Camino route goes L) to reach pensión.

Spanish students enjoying May Day on the Camino Inglés

SIGÜERO TO SANTIAGO

15.7km (9.8mi), ▲ 372M / ▼ 350M, ☻ 4-5 HOURS
🅿 69%, 10.8km / Ⓤ 31%, 4.9km, **DIFFICULTY:** ▬◻◻

Entering the Bosque Encantado "Enchanted Forest"

☼ Enjoy the final (short!) day into Santiago. With an early start, you may be able to even make noon mass at the Cathedral. Pass through a number of small villages on the way out of Sigüero and continue onto dirt roads to reach Formarís and the *Bosque Encantado* (Enchanted Forest). Soon reach the Tambre Industrial Park. Pay close attention to marks to navigate your way through suburban sprawl the rest of the way to the Santiago Cathedral.

4.6 Marantes 🛏🍴
🛏 **San Vicente** (€55+/65+): 🍴🛜◎▬, Marantes 12, ☎981694571 🗐, <u>+500m</u>

8.5 Formarís 🛏🍴
🛏 **Castro** (€35+/45+): 🍴🛜◎, Formarís 22-23, ☎981509304 🗐, pigrim discounts

12.3 Tambre 🛏🍴
🛏 **Pensión José Rey** (€20-23/40-45 🍽): 🛜◎, Tambre 80, ☎646665677 🗐
🛏 **Hospedaje Nosa Terra** (€20/30): 🍴🛜◎, Cruceiro Coruña 93, ☎981581389, <u>+400m</u>

15.7 Santiago de Compostela 🅰 🛏🍴🛒⌂◎✚🌐ⓘ🚉🅿🚉✈
See city map and accommodations list on p. 38-39.

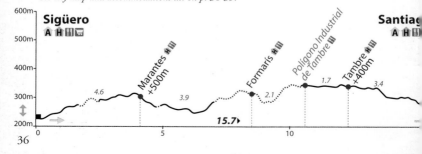

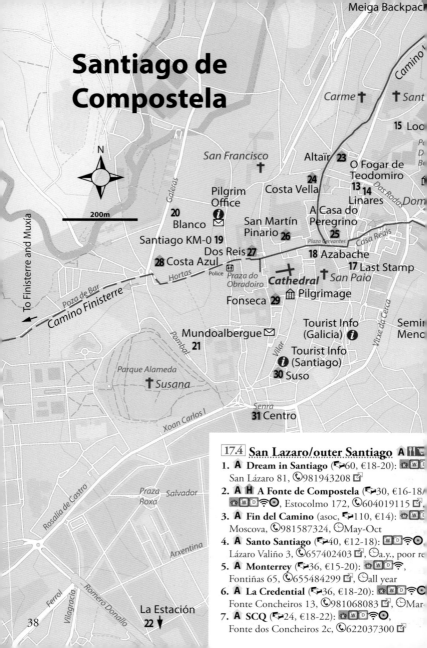

Santiago de Compostela

Meiga Backpac[k]

Camino

Carme † † Sant

15 Loo

San Francisco †

Altaïr 23

O Fogar de Teodomiro

24 Costa Vella

13 14

Pilgrim Office

Linares

20 Blanco

A Casa do Peregrino

Santiago KM-0 19

San Martín Pinario 26

25

18 Azabache

Dos Reis 27

Hortas

28 Costa Azul

Police

Praza do Obradoiro

17 Last Stamp

Cathedral † San Paio

Pilgrimage

Fonseca 29

To Finisterre and Muxia

Poza de Bar

Camino Finisterre

Galeras

Plaza Cervantes Casa Reás

Das Rodas Dom

Vixe da Cerca

Mundoalbergue 21

Pombal

Vilar

Tourist Info (Galicia)

Semi Meno

Tourist Info (Santiago)

30 Suso

Parque Alameda

† Susana

Senra

31 Centro

Xoan Carlos I

200m

N

Rosalia de Castro

Praza Roxa

Salvador

Arxentina

Ferrol Vilagracia Romeria Donallo

La Estación

22 ↓

38

Santo Santiago 4
San Lázaro
Dream in Santiago 1
Monterrey
5
Valiño
Camino Francés
2
A Fonte de Compostela
3
Fin del Camino
La Credential 6
Fontiñas
7 SCQ
8 Sixtos no Caminho
9 Santos
10 La Estrella de Santiago
Concheiros
Lugo
Roma
Parque de Carlomagno
Praza del Europa
11 Porta Real

antiago de Compostela A H

rim office: Rúa Carretas 33, 981568846, 9am-7pm (except Dec 25 & Jan 1),
iago city: Rúa do Vilar 63, 981555129, Daily 10am-6pm
cia: Plaza Mazarelos 15, 881866397, M-Sa 10am-5pm (closed Sundays)
Sixtos (40, €18-22/-/60): Fonte Concheiros 2, 881067936, Mar-Nov, no
Santos (24, €22/-/55): Concheiros 48, 881169386, Mar-Nov
Estrella de Santiago (24, €12-16): Concheiros 36-38, 881973926, all year
Meiga Backpackers (hostel, 30, €16-25): Basquiños 67, 981570846, all year
Fogar de Teodomiro (hstl, 20, €20-22): Algalia Arriba 3, 981582920
H **Linares** (14, €20-22/65/75): Algalia Abajo 34, 981580443
H **LoopINN** (€20-22/40-52/78): Tras de Santa Clara, 981585667
H **Seminario Menor** (177, €19/23/46): Quiroga Palacios 2, 881031768,
r-Oct, all beds not bunks, lockers available
Last Stamp (54, €20-25): Preguntoiro 10, 981563525, mid Jan-mid Dec
Azabache (20, €20-30): Azabachería 15, 981071254, all year
Santiago KM-0 (41, €20-35): das Carretas 11, 881974992
H **Blanco** (20, €15-20/40/50): Galeras 30, 881976850
Mundoalbergue (34, €19-22): San Clemente 26, 981588625, all year
La Estación (24, €15-17): Xoana Nogueira 14, 981594624, all year
Altaïr Hotel (€125-150): Loureiros 12, 981554712
Costa Vella (€80/110): Porta da Pena 17, 981569530, restored Jesuit house
A Casa Do Peregrino (€100): Azabacheria 2, 981573931
San Martín Pinario (pilgrim €25/40): Plaza Inmaculada 3, 981560282
Dos Reis Católicos (€280-350+): Praza do Obradoiro, 981582200, Parador
Costa Azul (€41/54-63): Das Galeras 18, 602451906
Pensión Fonseca (€70-80): Fonseca 1, 981584145
Hostal Suso (€80): Villar 65, 981586611
Pensión Centro (€40/55): Senra 11, 981588465

A CORUÑA TO SERGUDE

A1

20.0km (12.5mi), ▲ 600M / ▼ 485M, ☉ 5-6.5 HOURS
🅿 95%, 19.0km / Ⓤ 5%, 1.0km, **DIFFICULTY:** ▭▭▯

Plaza María Pita

☀ Take some time to enjoy A Coruña before setting out from Iglesia de Santiago. The city itself is beautiful, but much of the walking passes through urban/suburban sprawl. Towns thin out toward the end of day, offering some lovely views of the Galician countryside.

We've broken the A Coruña-Hospital de Bruma section into two short days to allow for both sightseeing in A Coruña and an early arrival in Hospital de Bruma (where beds can be scarce in the high season). If these days feel short, you can combine stages 1A and 2A into one long, challenging day (32.6km).

Navigation for this stage is a bit tricky with some poorly-marked turns, so we have included a more detailed written route description.

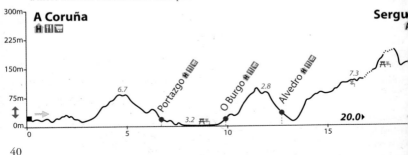

🏛 *Torre de Hércules*

A Coruña

0.0 **H** 🍴 🏪

Ría da Coruña

AG-13

Mera

Canide   Maianca

Dorneda

Abeleiras

A Silva

A Grela

Sta. Cruz

Coruxo

O Real

O Martinete

Mesoiro

Elviña

Perillo

Montrove

N-VI

Feáns

busy road! ⚠

Portazgo

6.7 **H** 🍴 🏪

difficult turn ⚠
6.3   🏪

pedestrian way

Burgo

Iñas

A Laxe

AC-211

Vilanova

Gándara

Corduzo

O Burgo

H 🍴 🏪

9.9

N-550

Barcala

AC-213

Zapateira

AC-14

Alvedro

H 🍴

12.7

Parque Empresarial

AC-214

Pravio

Cambre

Toroño

Tarrío

Mercadona 🏪

Santiago ✝

Mero

Meixigo

Orro

AC-400

Sésamo

Ledoño

O Drozo

16.4

Anceis

Suero

A-6

Andeiro

San Roque

Brexo

Vinxeira
Grande

🍴 *Da Cunha Pastelería*

Sergude

A 🍴

20.0

Celas

N-550

2 km

N

1   2

0.0   A Coruña A H 🍴🛒⛺🛏️➕✚ℹ️🏨♿✈️

A Coruña has been an important port city since the 2nd century (when the Romans arrived), and the Old City is built on Celtic fortifications that predate Roman times. Today A Coruña is a bustling metropolitan center—Galicia's second-largest city and a major economic center.

The impressive Torre de Hércules is well worth a visit, despite being far off route (~3km from Iglesia de Santiago). This 2nd-century lighthouse (renovated in 1791) is the oldest Roman lighthouse in use today (🕐Oct-May 10am-6pm, Jun-Sep 10am-9pm; €3, free on Mondays).

Iglesia de Santiago is a beautiful 12th-century Romanesque church. The figure of Santiago Matamoros on horseback adorns the west-facing entrance. Plaza María Pita is named for a Galician hero; she was famous for defending A Coruña against British invasion. In May 1589, with the city under siege by the British, Pita took up arms when her husband, an army captain, was killed in battle. Inspiring other women to join the fight, Pita helped drive back the British forces and claim victory in the defense of A Coruña. There are a number of interesting museums throughout the city—visit the main tourism office in Plaza María Pita for more information.

1. H **Hostal Alboran** (€32-41/47-67): 📶◐, Riego de Agua 14, 🕿981226579 📧
2. H **Hostal Hotil** (€25-35/30-60): 🍴📶, Galera 26-28, 🕿981976302 📧
3. H **Hostal Mara** (€20-50/28-55): 📶◐, Galera 49, 🕿981221802 📧
4. H **Hostal Carbonara** (€29+/35+): 📶◐, Nueva 16, 🕿981225251, 678503930 📧
5. H **Hostal La Provinciana** (€43-50/51-63): 📶◐, Nueva 7-9, 🕿981220400 📧
6. H **Pensión Roma** (€30/40): 🍴🅿📶, Nueva 3, 🕿981228075 📧
7. H **Hotel Lois** (€45-50/65-75): 🍴📶◐, Estrella 40, 🕿981212269 📧
8. H **Santa Catalina** (€30-42/45-60): 📶◐, Fernando Arenas Quintela 1, 🕿981226704/981226609 📧
9. H **Pensión Las Rías** (€25/30+): 🍴🅿📶, San Andrés 141, 🕿981226879/678503930 📧
10. H **Nido** (€27-43/39+ 🍴): 🍴🅿📶◐, San Andrés 146, 🕿981213201 📧
11. H **Maycar** (€30+/42+): 🍴🍴🅿📶◐, San Andrés 159, 🕿981226000 📧
12. H **Hostal Adelia** (€30+/40+): 🍴🍴🅿📶◐, Noya 29, 🕿981246849 📧
13. H **Hostal Palas** (€28/33): 📶◐, Marqués de Amboage 21, 🕿981247400 📧

From Iglesia de Santiago, cross through Plaza de Azcarraga and continue on Rúas Damas and Ángeles to Plaza María Pita, where an impressive palace houses the city hall. The tourism office is located to the R on the east edge of the Plaza (🕐Mon-Fri 9am-8:30pm, Sat 10am-8pm, Sun 10am-7pm). It's advisable to get a city map and navigational advice.

Continue straight through the Plaza, then follow Rúa Real to Rúa Cantón Grande (0.9km), a major road by the Jardines de Méndez Núñez. Continue along this major road (it becomes Avenida Linares Rivas). Continue parallel to the road as the sidewalk widens and the main road angles L. Cross Rúa Ramón de La Sagra (1.8km) and continue briefly along the main road, before turning L, crossing it, and following Av. Fernádez Latore as it angles R. Ahead at a Y, take the L option and not far beyond pass the central bus station on your R (2.8km).

At a traffic circle with metal sculpture in the middle (3.2km), turn L following Avenida d Monelos uphill. Stay on this road for several kilometers (name changes to Estrada Eirís an Avenida de Montserrat). As you climb the hill, pass an Eroski supermarket and descend o the other side. At the bottom, ⚠ exercise extreme caution as you cross several highway ex and entrance ramps on the way to/from a bridge crossing motorway AC-11 (5.8km).

⚠ Half a kilometer ahead (6.3km) you reach a tricky turn: immediately after Pulpería L Arboleda and Restaurante O Pincho, turn L onto a small side street, descending into Portazg and the waterfront. There are few marks in this area, some have been erased and some incor rectly point straight, so keep an eye out for the restaurant landmarks.

6.7 Portazgo ⊞⫼🛒➕€

⊞ Hotel A Barquiña (€33+/55+ 🛏): ⫼🛜⊘, Plaza de Santa Gema 7, ☎981662402 ⬚

⊞ Hotel Crunia (€50+/55+): ⫼ⓌⒹ🛜⊘, Fonteculler 58, ☎981650088/619413412 ⬚

Once in Portazgo (6.7km), cross the main road (AC-211) and a bridge over the railroa tracks. On the other side of the bridge, turn R and descend to a paved pedestrian path an follow it along the river. Reach the new and old bridges of O Burgo (AC-211 and the ol stone bridge that is now a monument) and turn R into town, soon passing Iglesia de Santiag (9.8km) on the R.

9.9 O Burgo ⊞⫼🛒⊙➕€🚌🏧

Iglesia de Santiago is on the western side of the Ría do Burgo bridge. This Romanesque church dates to the 12th century, but because of modern renovations, little of the original Romanesque style remains. Iglesia de Santa María is across the river.

⊞ Residencial La Poetisa (€45+/60+): 🛜, Enrique Tierno Galván 24, ☎981665871/686287506 ⬚

⊞ Hostal El Mesón (€21/37): 🛜, Coruña 25, ☎98166006

At a Y, turn L, then take the following L at a traffic circle. Pass under AP-9, following AC-213; then take a R (10.5km), leaving the main road and ascending through several small villages.

Descend to the Parque Empresarial de Alvedro (12.3km) and walk south on a sidewalk parallel to N-550 until you reach a traffic circle and turn L (13.1km).

12.7 Alvedro H ⛨ 🛒

The Mercadona grocery store at the traffic circle at the south edge of the industrial park is the last on-route grocery store until Sergude. Iglesia de Santiago de Sigrás (14.1km) is 1.4km past Alvedro. This Romanesque church dates to the 12th century with significant renovations made over its history. Today the building has elements of Gothic, Renaissance, Baroque, and Neoclassical styles. The interior chapel walls and chapel arch are original.

H Pensión La Paz (€18/28): ⛨ 🛜, Alvedro 41, 📞981650101

Follow an unpaved path through a park/grassy area and across a stream and continue on pavement. Pass Iglesia de Santiago de Sigrás (14.1km) and continue climbing to O Drozo (16.4km). Not far ahead, pass a bakery (Da Cunha, 18.3km) and shaded rest area with picnic tables and a water fountain (18.7km), before reaching the Sergude Xunta albergue (20.0km).

20.0 Sergude A ⛨

The bar in town (400m past albergue) serves good meals and sells very basic food/groceries.

A Xunta (🛏30, €8): 🏧 W D 🛜 ⊙, CP-2103 1, 📞646728143, 🕐1-10pm all year, clean, pleasant, in peaceful location; limited cookware in kitchen

Fountain in O Drozo (left)

Galician countryside before Presedo provides a welcome respite from urban walking

SERGUDE TO BRUMA

12.6km (7.9mi), ▲ 491M / ▼ 234M, ⏱ 3.5-5 HOURS
🅿 57%, 7.2km / Ⓤ 43%, 5.4km, **DIFFICULTY:** ▬☐☐

Fields outside of Presedo

☀ Leave the outskirts of A Coruña completely behind as you continue into Galician farmland. The day is short but has a long, demanding climb on the way to the Hospital de Bruma, a historical pilgrim hostel, where you'll meet pilgrims walking the Camino Inglés from Ferrol. If you're ambitious, continue another 24.5km to Sigüero.

`3.1` Sarandóns Ⓗ🍴

Ⓗ **Casa das Veigas** (€75+ 🍴): 🍴🛜☀▤, Sarandóns 1, ☎981671616/663320984 📧, **+550m** from south end of town

`12.6` Bruma Ⓐ🍴, see p. 31

`24.8` Mesón do Vento Ⓗ🍴🛒➕€🍴, +1.7km, see p. 31

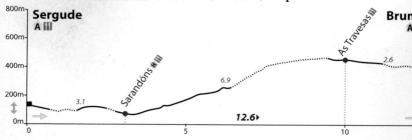

Sergude 0.0

A 🍴

*Polígono Industrial
Os Capelos*

San Roque

Ameás

Barcés

A Bailía 2.2

Carral

S. Juan ✝ **Sarandóns**
3.1 🍴

Ardexurxe

H *Casa das Vegas*
✝ *Sta. María*

Abegondo

AC-542

Montouto

Barcés

Herves

N-550

Corredoira

AP-9

Argonte

Canedo

As Travesas 🍴 ⛩
10.0

*Stage 4:
Betanzos to
Bruma*

**Mesón do
Vento,**
+1.7km
H 🍴 🛒

AC-542

Bruma 12.6
A 🍴

*City map on
Stage 4 map*

N

1 km

0   0.5   1

About the Authors

Matthew Harms is a walker and cyclist, at heart a traveler wh[o] believes in slower forms of transportation that allow for a clos[er] understanding of people, communities, and landscapes. He spe[nt] many years in the Balkans and Middle East, helping to develo[p] hiking routes in both regions. He has traveled thousands of miles o[f] foot and by bike in the Middle East, Europe, and the United State[s] and he is currently based in Colorado, where he works as a nurs[e] when not traveling or exploring the Rocky Mountains.

Anna Dintaman & **David Landis** are the cofounders of Villag[e] to Village Press and bring over 15 years of experience workin[g] with trails in Europe, the Middle East, Asia, and their home are[a] in the Shenandoah Valley of Virginia. Avid hikers and cyclist[s] their experiences range from backpacking Patagonia and Nepa[l] to hiking in the Middle East and biking across the USA. Davi[d] cofounded the Jesus Trail, a hiking trail in the Galilee, and devel[-] oped the TransVirginia gravel bikepacking route. They have share[d] a deep love for the Camino since they first took a 500-mile journe[y] on the Camino Francés. They enjoy introducing their children t[o] the joys of the outdoors and learning from other cultures.

Feedback welcome: info@villagetovillagepress.com

 facebook.com/caminoguidebooks

 instagram.com/caminoguidebook

Village to Village Press specializes in publishing guidebooks and supporting trail development projects worldwide.

CaminoGuidebook.com

Visit for free planning information including easy online booking, digital interactive maps, GPS tracks for navigation and frequently asked questions.

Kindle versions also available

VILLAGE TO VILLAGE PRESS
WWW.VILLAGETOVILLAGEPRESS.COM